☐ Take five steps forward. Color the space green.

☐ Go forward three steps. Draw a yellow circle around the letter.

☐ Go back two steps. Color the space blue.

☐ Take six forward steps. Put a red X on the letter.

☐ Go backwards two steps. Draw a purple square.

☐ Color the boy's shirt red.

- [ ] Put a black hat on the snowman.
- [ ] Draw a tree by the ice skater.
- [ ] Put ski poles in the skier's hands.
- [ ] Make a person on the snowmobile.
- [ ] Draw a red line from the sled to the ice skater.
- [ ] Draw an orange line from the snowman to the snowmobile.

Homework Helpers
Reading Grade 2

As a parent, you want your child to enjoy learning and to do well in school. The activities in the *Homework Helpers* series will help your child develop the skills and self-confidence that lead to success. Humorous illustrations and diverse formats make the activities interesting for your child.

HOW TO USE THIS BOOK

- Provide a quiet, comfortable place to work with your child.

- Plan a special time to work with your child. Create a warm, accepting atmosphere so your child will enjoy spending this time with you. Limit each session to one or two activities.

- Make sure your child understands the directions before beginning an activity.

- Check the answers with your child as soon as an activity has been completed. (Be sure to remove the answer pages from the center of the book before your child uses the book.)

- The activities in this book were selected from previously published Frank Schaffer materials.

- Topics covered in this book are color and number words, sight words, opposite words, classification, following directions, and comprehension skills such as sequencing, finding facts, drawing conclusions, and making inferences.

ISBN #0-86734-104-1

FS-8137 Homework Helpers—Reading Grade 2
All rights reserved—Printed in the U.S.A.
Copyright © 1991 Frank Schaffer Publications, Inc.
23740 Hawthorne Blvd., Torrance, CA 90505

This book or parts thereof may not be reproduced in any form or mechanically stored in any retrieval system without written permission from the publisher.

This Book Belongs To

Name _____

Date _____

Follow Directions!

☐ Draw a purple hat for the dog.

☐ Make a yellow sun.

☐ Put a green fish on the fishing line.

☐ Color the water blue.

☐ Give the dog three orange spots.

☐ Draw two blue birds in the sky.

Do what each sentence tells you to do.

☐ Put a red X on the car.

☐ Put a blue circle around Mary's house.

☐ Draw a green line from Bill's house to Tom's house.

☐ Draw a brown line from Mary's house to Bill's house.

☐ Draw a black line from Tom's house to the Fire Station.

The Circus Parade

Here comes the circus parade. First come the clowns. Next, the band marches by. Now a gray elephant slowly goes past us. A brown bear is walking on two legs. At the end of the parade we will see the monkeys.

1. What are we watching?
   _____

2. What comes first?
   _____

3. What comes next?
   _____

4. How is the bear walking?
   _____

5. What will be at the end of the parade?
   _____

6. Make a picture about the first sentence.

Compound Words

Use two words from the list to make one **compound** word for each sentence.

day	class	plane
cow	grand	birth
air	room	mother
pop	door	place
bed	base	room
boy	bell	ball
corn	fire	

1. A _____ rides on a horse.

2. I sleep in my _____.

3. Did you ring the _____?

4. Ann will be 7 on her _____.

5. You can fly in an _____.

6. Please put butter on the _____.

7. Our _____ team won the game.

8. There are 14 girls in our _____.

9. Put the wood in the _____.

10. My _____ lives next door.

A Dog On A Bus

A dog got on a bus. The bus went fast. It went to the park. The dog got off the bus. He met his mother in the park. She gave him a dog bone. It tasted good!

1. Who took a ride on the bus?
   _____

2. How did the bus go?
   _____

3. Where did the bus go?
   _____

4. Who did the dog see?
   _____

5. What did the dog eat?
   _____

6. How did it taste?
   _____

7. Make a picture about this story.

Synonyms

a. big
b. touch
c. talk
d. unhappy
e. save
f. auto
g. hope
h. small
i. sick
j. stone
k. kind
l. all
m. close
n. sniff
o. pot

Write the letter of the word that means the same.

____ 1. sad
____ 2. wish
____ 3. shut
____ 4. large
____ 5. ill
____ 6. rock
____ 7. nice
____ 8. feel
____ 9. speak
____ 10. car
____ 11. smell
____ 12. every
____ 13. keep
____ 14. pan
____ 15. little

Number these pictures in order from 1-6.

Antonyms — Opposites

wet	slow	close	play
hot	thin	float	first
go	hard	black	under
new	short	dirty	night

Write the word that means the opposite.

1. dry _____
2. clean _____
3. tall _____
4. cold _____
5. fast _____
6. thick _____
7. white _____
8. over _____

9. sink _____
10. day _____
11. work _____
12. last _____
13. soft _____
14. old _____
15. stop _____
16. open _____

My Dog

I love my dog. My dog loves me. He likes me to rub his belly. He likes me to feed him cheese. He loves to sleep in my bed. He likes to be brushed. I'm so lucky to have him for a pet.

1. Why am I lucky?
   _____

2. Does my dog like to be brushed?
   _____

3. Who is my pet?
   _____

4. Who loves me?
   _____

5. Name three things my pet likes.
   _____

6. Make a picture about the fifth sentence.

Homonyms

Write the **correct** word for each sentence.

| maid |
| made |

1. The _____ cleaned the house.
2. I _____ my bed.

| son |
| sun |

3. The boy is my _____.
4. The _____ is hot today.

| here |
| hear |

5. She can't _____ you.
6. You may sit _____.

| meet |
| meat |

7. Dad will buy some _____.
8. Adam can _____ you at school.

| blew |
| blue |

9. The wind really _____.
10. Jim likes the color _____.

Sources of Heat

Find out about the many different ways we get heat. Look at these pictures. Then write a sentence about a source of heat by unscrambling each group of words. Remember to use capitals and periods!

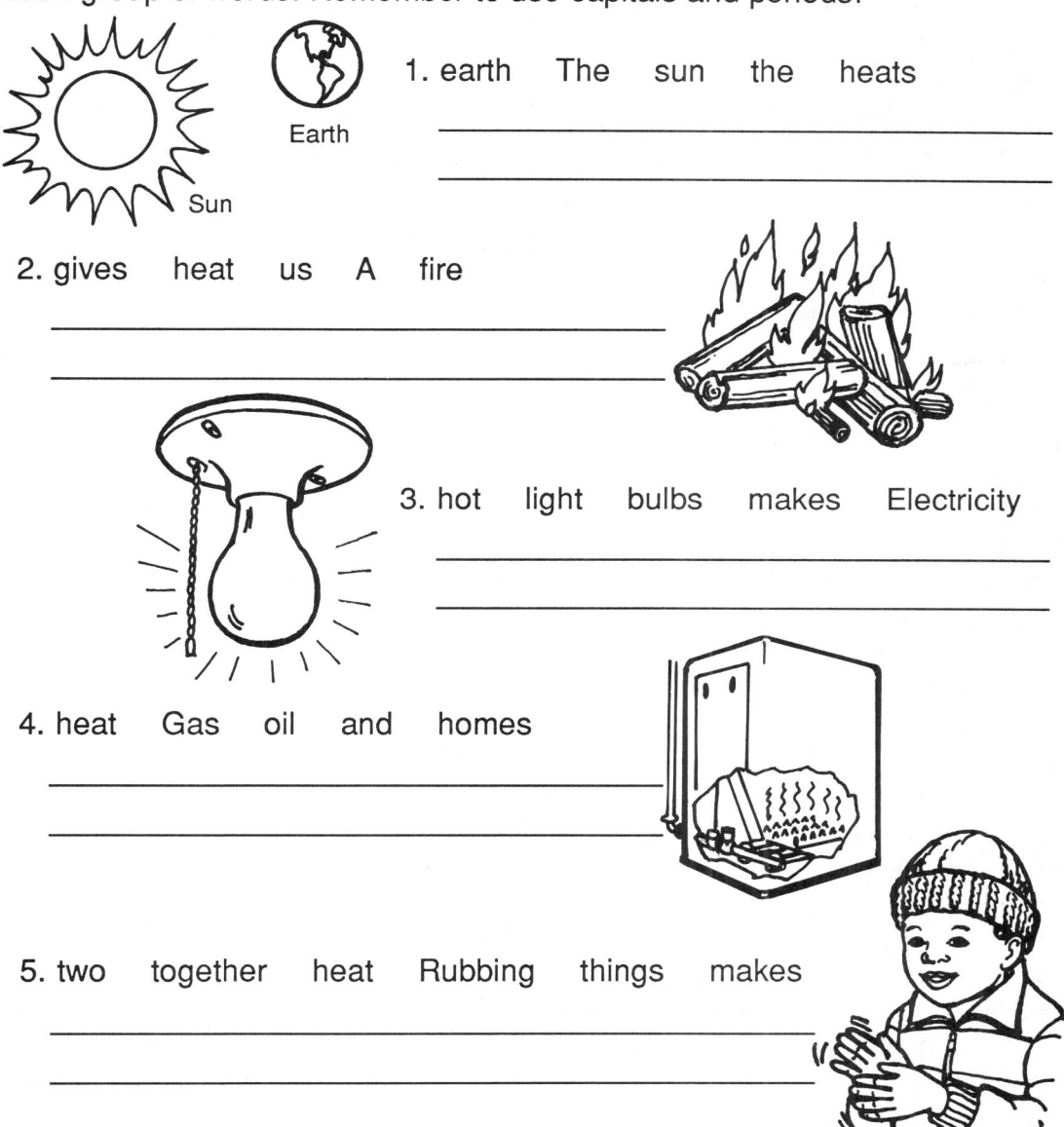

1. earth   The   sun   the   heats

2. gives   heat   us   A   fire

3. hot   light   bulbs   makes   Electricity

4. heat   Gas   oil   and   homes

5. two   together   heat   Rubbing   things   makes

Try This! Heat is used for cooking. List three other uses for heat.

Circle the two words that make each contraction.

1.	we'll	she will	we will	we are
2.	can't	can not	had not	she is
3.	you've	you have	I have	you will
4.	I'm	I will	he is	I am
5.	you'll	you have	you will	he will
6.	they've	they will	we have	they have
7.	what's	you are	he is	what is
8.	we're	we are	we will	you are
9.	let's	he is	let us	I am
10.	couldn't	she is	has not	could not

Why Does . . . ?

Let's match words. Jar goes with glass because a jar is made from glass. Now...bat goes with ball...left goes with right...mouse goes with cheese...paper goes with book... and water goes with fish.

Did you say cheese?

1. Why does jar go with glass?
   _____

2. Why does bat go with ball?
   _____

3. Why does left go with right?
   _____

4. Why does mouse go with cheese?
   _____

5. Why does paper go with book?
   _____

6. Why does water go with fish?
   _____

7. Name two other things that go together.
   _____

Beautiful Butterflies

Number each group of words in alphabetical order.

Example

___3___ blue
___2___ big
___1___ ball

A.
____ wax
____ who
____ would

B.
____ pond
____ pull
____ park

C.
____ rake
____ rook
____ ride

D.
____ us
____ under
____ up

E.
____ after
____ about
____ away

F.
____ of
____ old
____ own

A Nice Day

It's a nice day to take a walk. I'll ask my friend Jimmy to go with me. We'll play ball at the park. Maybe we'll fly kites. The wind is strong. When it starts getting dark, we will hurry home.

1. What will I do?
   _____

2. Who will go with me?
   _____

3. Where will we go?
   _____

4. What will we do at the park?
   _____

5. What is strong?
   _____

6. When will we go home?
   _____

Busy Bees

Number each group of words in alphabetical order.

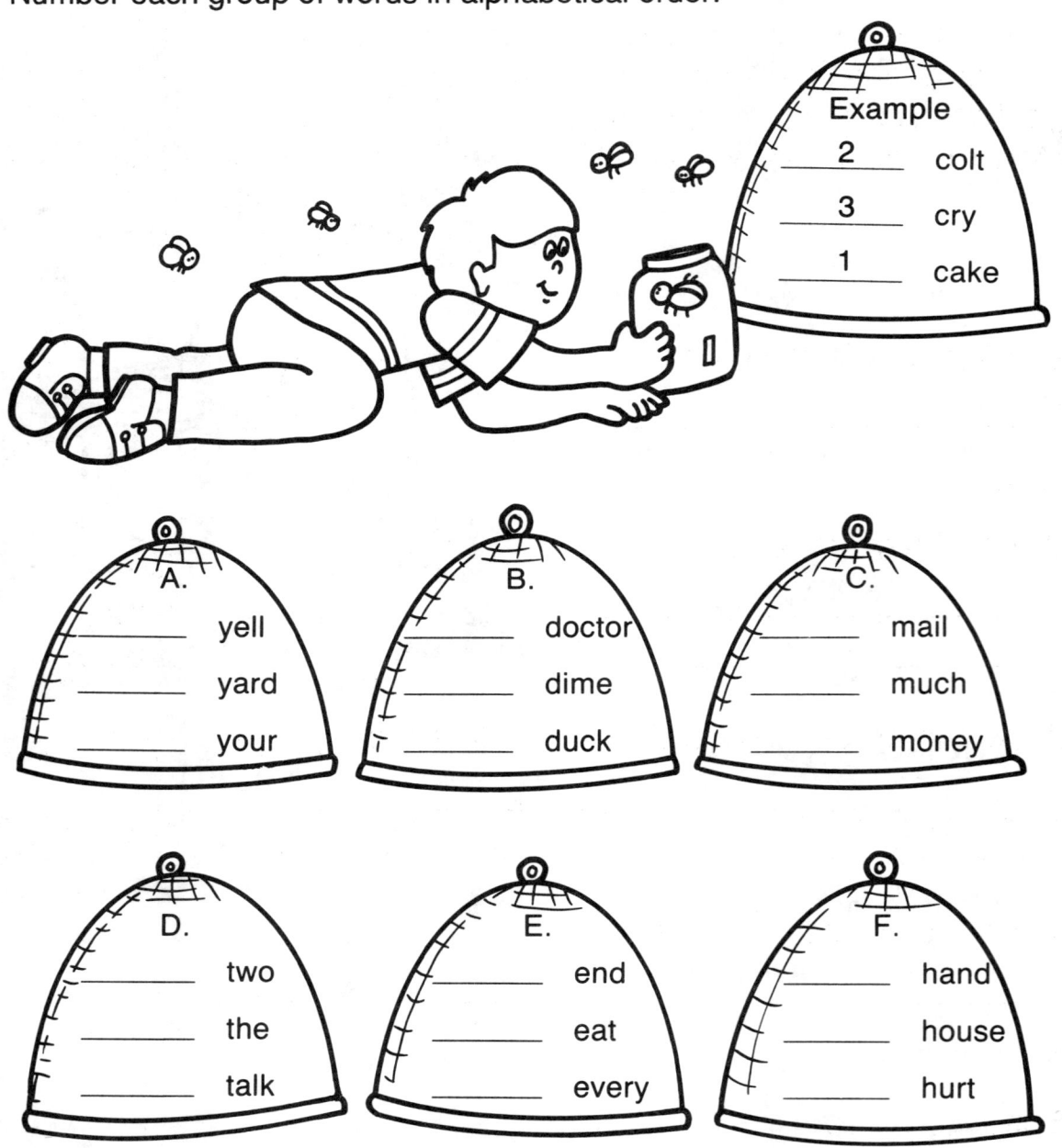

Example
2 colt
3 cry
1 cake

A.
___ yell
___ yard
___ your

B.
___ doctor
___ dime
___ duck

C.
___ mail
___ much
___ money

D.
___ two
___ the
___ talk

E.
___ end
___ eat
___ every

F.
___ hand
___ house
___ hurt

Monsters

I am reading such a good book. It is about monsters. These monsters are very nice. They play baseball, eat ice cream and go to school. These monsters even have brothers and sisters. Monsters only live in books, you know. Let's keep it that way!

1. Who is this story about?
   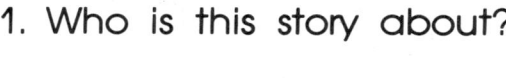

2. Are they good or bad?

3. Name three things that monsters do?

4. Where is the only place that monsters live?
   _____

5. Make a picture of the monsters in the story.

Go-Togethers

Write the three words that go together in each row.

Clouds

I like to sit on the grass and look at the sky. So many beautiful clouds float by. I play a game. I give each cloud a name. Here comes a cloud that looks like a horse. Here comes a butterfly cloud. Now a flower cloud is floating past me. It would be such fun to float like a cloud!

1. What is green in this story?

2. What is the game?

3. Name three clouds in this story.

4. What would be such fun?

5. Make a picture of the clouds.

Which Ones?

Circle the right answers for each question.

1. Which ones are workers?

   nurse   barber   pilot   carpenter   puppy

2. Which ones are parts of a house?

   grass   door   window   wall   roof

3. What would you find in a forest?

   trees   whale   chipmunk   pine cones   deer

4. Which ones are time words?

   day   year   penny   month   week

5. Which ones are trees?

   pine   elm   oak   daisy   spruce

6. Which ones live in the ocean?

   seal   pig   shark   octopus   whale

7. Which ones are countries?

   Japan   U.S.A.   Canada   Kansas   Mexico

8. Which ones are directions?

   far   north   east   south   west

9. In which ones could you ride?

   car   truck   wagon   boat   stove

10. Which ones are too heavy to carry?

    elephant   feather   house   car   cow

11. Which ones can you wear?

    pants   coat   shirt   lamp   shoes

12. Which ones measure something?

    ruler   teaspoon   purse   cup   yardstick

A Mouse In Our House

There's a mouse in our house. We can't find it. We have never seen it. It eats our cheese. It makes noise at night. It makes our cat run all over the house. I hear it under my bed at night. Some day I'll see that mouse. Until then, I'll call it — Mr. Invisible!

1. Who is this story about?
   _____

2. Where does the mouse live?
   _____

3. What does it eat?
   _____

4. What does the cat do?
   _____

5. Where can you hear the mouse at night?
   _____

6. What is the mouse's name?
   _____

Dive In

Write the name of the category at the top of each box.

milk
punch
tea

house
tent
igloo

jump
skip
swim

door
roof
window

shark
whale
seal

Pull-Out Answers

Remove these answer pages before your child uses the book.

Pull-Out Answers

Pages One to Four
self-explanatory

Page Five
1. a circus parade
2. the clowns
3. the band
4. on two legs
5. the monkeys

Page Six
1. cowboy
2. bedroom
3. doorbell
4. birthday
5. airplane
6. popcorn
7. baseball
8. classroom
9. fireplace
10. grandmother

Page Seven
1. a dog
2. fast
3. to the park
4. his mother
5. a bone
6. good

Page Eight
1. d
2. g
3. m
4. a
5. i
6. j
7. k
8. b
9. c
10. f
11. n
12. l
13. e
14. o
15. h

Page Nine
3 6
5 1
2 4

Page Ten
1. wet
2. dirty
3. short
4. hot
5. slow
6. thin
7. black
8. under
9. float
10. night
11. play
12. first
13. hard
14. new
15. go
16. close

Page Eleven
1. because I have a pet
2. yes
3. my dog
4. my dog
5. to have his belly rubbed, to eat cheese, to be brushed

Page Twelve
1. maid
2. made
3. son
4. sun
5. hear
6. here
7. meat
8. meet
9. blew
10. blue

Page Thirteen
1. The sun heats the earth.
2. A fire gives us heat.
3. Electricity makes light bulbs hot.
4. Gas and oil heat homes.
5. Rubbing two things together makes heat.

Page Fourteen
1. we will
2. can not
3. you have
4. I am
5. you will
6. they have
7. what is
8. we are
9. let us
10. could not

Page Fifteen
1. A jar is made from glass.
2. They are used together.
3. They are opposites.
4. Mice like cheese.
5. A book is made of paper.
6. Fish swim in water.
7. Answers vary.

Page Sixteen
A. 1, 2, 3
B. 2, 3, 1
C. 1, 3, 2
D. 3, 1, 2
E. 2, 1, 3
F. 1, 2, 3

Page Seventeen
1. take a walk
2. my friend Jimmy
3. to the park
4. play ball
5. the wind
6. when it starts getting dark

Page Eighteen
A. 2, 1, 3
B. 2, 1, 3
C. 1, 3, 2
D. 3, 2, 1
E. 2, 1, 3
F. 1, 2, 3

Pull-Out Answers

Page Nineteen
1. monsters
2. good
3. play baseball, eat ice cream, go to school
4. in books

Page Twenty
1. iron, stove, fire
2. wheel, penny, ball
3. man's hat, bonnet, hood
4. safe, piggy bank, wallet

Page Twenty-one
1. grass
2. giving clouds names
3. horse, butterfly, flower
4. to float like a cloud

Page Twenty-two
1. nurse, barber, pilot, carpenter
2. door, window, wall, roof
3. trees, chipmunk, pine cones, deer
4. day, year, month, week
5. pine, elm, oak, spruce
6. seal, shark, octopus, whale
7. Japan, U.S.A., Canada, Mexico
8. north, east, south, west
9. car, truck, wagon, boat
10. elephant, house, car, cow
11. pants, coat, shirt, shoes
12. ruler, teaspoon, cup, yardstick

Page Twenty-three
1. a mouse
2. in our house
3. cheese
4. runs all over the house
5. under my bed
6. Mr. Invisible

Page Twenty-four
Answers vary.

Page Twenty-five
Answers must be in complete sentences that include this information.
1. decides which clothes to take
2. folds her clothes
3. packs her suitcase
4. puts her suitcase in the car
5. gets in the car
6. waves good-bye

Page Twenty-six
1. chalk, desks, paints, erasers, pencils, paper, scissors
2. cake, candy, gifts, suckers, candles, nut cups, ice cream
3. harp, tuba, drums, flute, piano, guitar, cymbals

Page Twenty-seven
1. boy—girl
2. yes—no, run—walk, go—stop
3. down
4. Answers vary.

Page Twenty-eight
1. Bread
2. Sports
3. Boats
4. States
5. Fruit
6. Planets
7. Musical Instruments
8. Dogs

Page Twenty-nine
1. ten o'clock
2. Jimmy
3. wet sand
4. car
5. The sand doesn't fall down.

Page Thirty
1. apartment
2. harbor
3. telephone
4. blaze
5. feast
6. skates
7. sack
8. library

Page Thirty-one
1. ill
2. begin
3. chop
4. happy
5. go
6. nice
7. little
8. pretty
9. yell
10. feel

Page Thirty-two
1. bubblegum
2. I blew a bubble.
3. It pulled me into the air.
4. You should be careful.

Page Thirty-three
1. one time
2. foot
3. over
4. around
5. two
6. keep
7. make
8. must

Page Thirty-four
1. cold
2. soon
3. thank
4. happy
5. When
6. off
7. fast
8. gave

Pull-Out Answers

Page Thirty-five
Answers must be in complete sentences that include this information.
1. flew off the tree branch
2. landed on the ground
3. picked up a twig in her beak
4. flew back to the tree with the twig and put it in her nest
5. added a few more twigs
6. laid two beautiful blue eggs

Page Thirty-six
1. anyone
2. smooth
3. They bounce back toward you.
4. They break up sound waves.
5. where there are mountains all around

Page Thirty-seven
1. First, Juan got the popcorn popper out of the cupboard.
2. Second, he added the popcorn.
3. Third, he put a bowl under the popper's spout.
4. Next, he plugged in the popper.
5. Then, he turned on the switch.
6. After that, he watched the corn pop.
7. Finally, he ate the popcorn.

Page Thirty-eight
Forest
   porcupines, owls, mice, chipmunks, black bears
Desert
   kangaroo rats, lizards, scorpions, roadrunners, sidewinder rattlesnakes

Page Thirty-nine
1. crib
2. water
3. head
4. tree
5. rabbit

Page Forty
1. Riding a Seahorse
2. Mice Like Cheese
3. A Skater's Bad Fall
4. The Skating Turtle

Page Forty-one
1. b
2. a
3. c

Page Forty-two
1. b
2. a
3. a
4. b

Page Forty-three
1. no
2. yes
3. yes
4. no
5. no
6. no
7. yes
8. no
9. yes
10. yes

Page Forty-four
1. camel
2. shark
3. giraffe
4. lion
5. zebra

Page Forty-five
1. a
2. b
3. b

Page Forty-six
1. soft
2. hook
3. A sticky subject
4. A bear gets stuck with a quill.
5. but it can take care of itself.

Page Forty-seven
1. oil
2. by his tail
3. when he is scared
4. Answer varies.
5. its oil sac has been removed

Page Forty-eight
1. night
2. clearly
3. light
4. before
5. flame
6. eyes
7. travels
8. tree
9. lamp
10. book

Get Ready, Set, Go!

Help Julie get ready to go to camp. Use the phrases to write sentences that show the order in which she should do these things.

1. _____
2. _____
3. _____
4. _____
   _____
5. _____
6. _____

Brainwork! Write in order five things that Julie might do when she arrives at camp.

Write each word from the word box under the right category.

1. Classroom	2. Birthday Things	3. Musical Instruments

Word Box

cake	drums	desks	piano	suckers	cymbals	scissors
harp	candy	gifts	paints	erasers	paper	nut cups
tuba	chalk	flute	guitar	pencils	candles	ice cream

Opposites

Did you know that the opposite of boy is girl? The opposite of yes is no. The opposite of run is walk. The opposite of go is stop. But, the opposite of up is not high.

1. What are the opposite words in the first sentence?
   _____

2. What are the other opposite word pairs?
   _____

3. What should the opposite be in the last sentence?
   _____

4. List three pairs of opposites.
   _____

Write the name of the category at the **top** of each box.
Then write two more things that belong to each category.

1.	2.	3.
white rye whole wheat _____ _____	surfing ice skating basketball _____ _____	sailboat raft canoe _____ _____
4.	**5.**	**6.**
Maryland Alabama Kentucky _____ _____	apples oranges plums _____ _____	Saturn Neptune Pluto _____ _____
7.	**8.**	
piano violin flute _____ _____	poodle cocker spaniel collie _____ _____	

The Playground

At school when the ten o'clock bell rings, we hurry out to recess. It's fun to see my friend Jimmy on the playground. We both start digging in the sand. We are making a track for our toy cars. We have found that wet sand is better to work with; the sand doesn't fall down. You really learn a lot on the playground!

1. What time is recess?
   _____

2. Who is my friend?
   _____

3. What is the track made of?
   _____

4. Name a toy in this story.
   _____

5. Why is wet sand good?
   _____

What Is It?

apartment	feast	telephone	skates
harbor	blaze	sack	library

Write the correct word on each line.

1. It is a place to live.

2. This is a place for boats.

3. You can call someone on this.

4. This is a big fire.

5. This is a big dinner.

6. These have wheels.

7. This is like a paper bag.

8. You can find books here.

Circle the word that means about the same as the underlined word.

1. sick	door	ill	well
2. start	begin	end	kite
3. cut	blow	lock	chop
4. glad	swim	happy	sad
5. leave	go	wish	come
6. kind	ship	rich	nice
7. small	large	little	soft
8. beautiful	pretty	ugly	vote
9. shout	spot	quiet	yell
10. touch	feel	see	woods

Bubblegum

Once I chewed a stick of bubblegum. I started to blow a bubble. It got bigger and bigger. It pulled me into the air. I was going up in the sky. Be very careful when you chew a stick of bubblegum.

1. What did I chew?
   _____

2. Then what did I do?
   _____

3. What did the bubble do with me?
   _____

4. What should you do when you chew bubblegum?
   _____

5. Make a picture about this story.

What Does It Mean?

Circle the best answer for each question.

1. I will only say it **once**.
   What does **once** mean?
   carefully   one time   today

2. My cat got a sticker in her **paw**.
   What does **paw** mean?
   head   foot   eye

3. He drove **across** the bridge.
   What does **across** mean?
   by   under   over

4. Dad paid **about** $100.00 for it.
   What does **about** mean?
   around   under   me

5. **Both** of us will go with you.
   What does **both** mean?
   one   two   none

6. I will **save** the old toys for us.
   What does **save** mean?
   keep   throw   run

7. Will you **draw** a picture?
   What does **draw** mean?
   get   blow   make

8. I **have to** go home now.
   What does **have to** mean?
   stay   swim   must

Snow!

Circle the right word for each sentence.

1. It is really | call | cold | today.
2. We will go | soon | sleep |
3. Please | think | thank | them for us.
4. I am | very | happy | for you.
5. | When | Would | are they going home?
6. Will you please turn the oven | off | or | ?
7. How | fast | first | can you run?
8. Dad | gave | goes | us some money.

Rachel Robin

First Rachel Robin flew off the tree branch. Next she landed on the ground. Then she picked up a twig in her beak. After that she flew back to the tree with the twig and put it in her nest. Later she added a few more twigs. Finally she laid two beautiful blue eggs.

Write a complete sentence to answer each question.

1. What did Rachel do **first**? _____

2. What did Rachel do **next**? _____

3. What did Rachel do **then**? _____

4. What did Rachel do **after** that? _____

5. What did Rachel do **later**? _____

6. What did Rachel do **finally**? _____

Brainwork! Write what will happen next. Draw a picture.

Echoes

Have you ever heard your own words come back at you? That's an echo! If you shout at a hard, smooth surface, the sound waves will bounce back toward you. Something rough will not work because a rough surface breaks up sound waves.

   Try it yourself. Stand at least 60 feet away from a wall, if you want a good echo. Then yell! The best place to make echoes is where there are mountains all around you. The sound will echo many times. Try sending a message.

Write in the correct answers about echoes.

1. Who can make an echo?
   _____

2. What kind of surface do you need?
   _____

3. What happens to the sound waves when you shout?
   _____

4. Why don't rough surfaces work?
   _____

5. Where is the best place to make an echo?
   _____

POP Goes the Popcorn!

Help Juan pop the popcorn. Read the mixed-up paragraph and number the sentences in the right order. Then make a paragraph by writing the sentences in order.

_____ Third, he put a bowl under the popper's spout.

_____ After that, he watched the corn pop. _____ Then, he turned on the switch. _____ Finally, he ate the popcorn.

___1___ First, Juan got the popcorn popper out of the cupboard.

_____ Next, he plugged in the popper. _____ Second, he added the popcorn.

_____

_____

_____

_____

_____

_____

_____

_____

Brainwork! Write three things Juan did to clean up after he finished making popcorn.

Forest or Desert Habitat

Forest

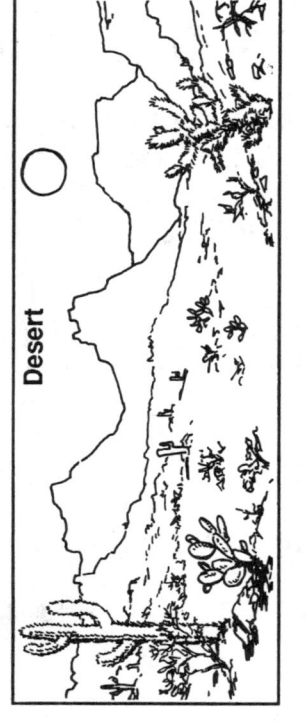
Desert

The forest is the habitat of many animals. A habitat is the place where an animal lives in nature. Forests have many trees, bushes, and caves that provide animals with hiding places, food, and homes. **Porcupines** munch on tender twigs. At night **owls** catch **mice** that are looking for seeds and nuts. In the winter **chipmunks** live in burrows and eat stored seeds and nuts, while **black bears** sleep in their dens.

Desert animals are well suited to life in their hot, dry habitat. **Kangaroo rats** get water from the seeds and roots of desert plants. **Lizards** eat insects and birds' eggs. **Scorpions** have a thick skin that protects them from the heat. **Roadrunners** find water at scattered water holes. **Sidewinder rattlesnakes** hunt at night when the desert is cooler.

Write the name of each animal under the picture of its habitat.

Try This! Write the names and habitats of ten animals that live in the forest or desert.

What's Missing?

Each group of pictures must go together in the same way. Write the missing word. Use the word box.

Word Box				
head	crib	rabbit	tree	water

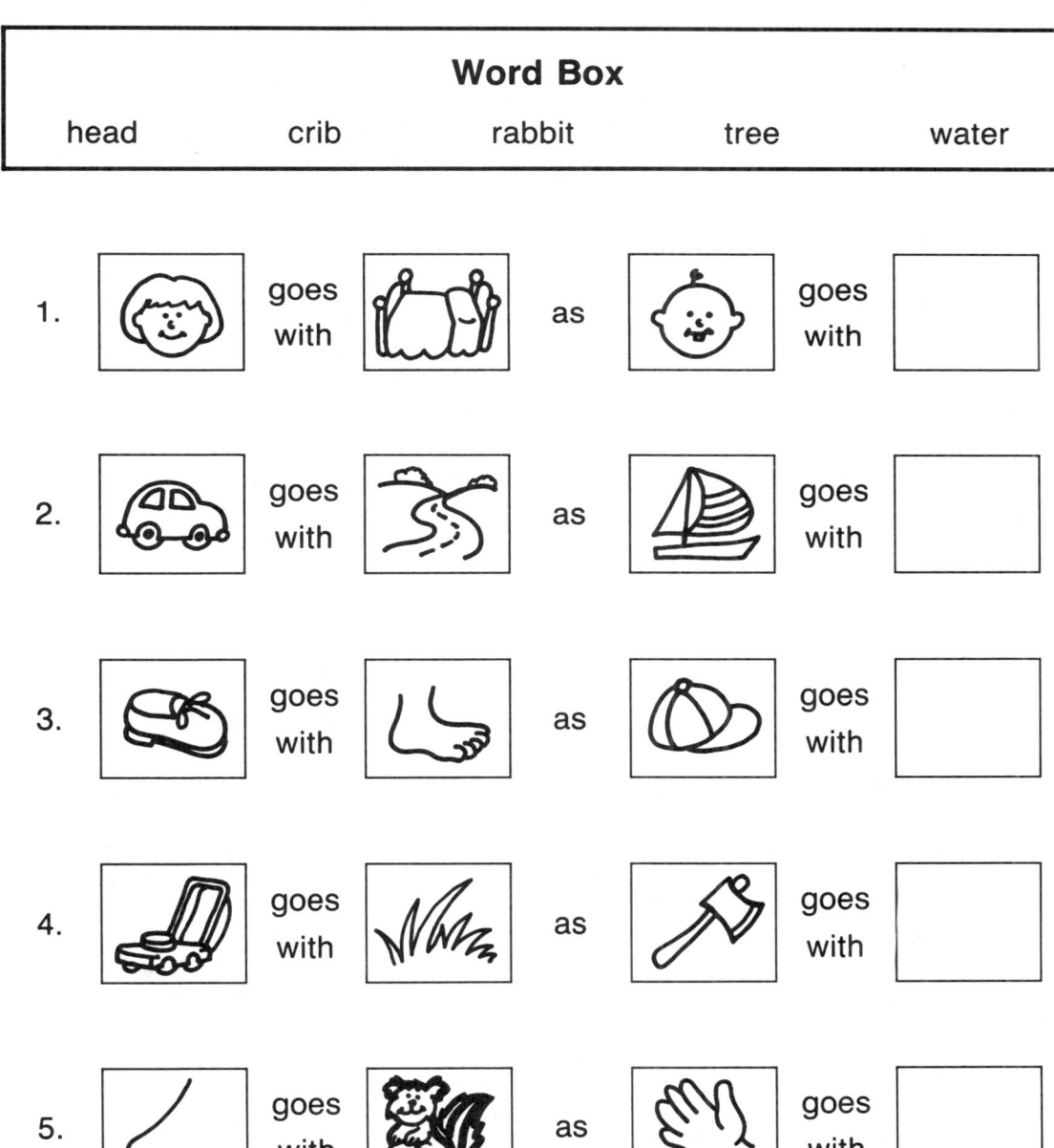

Find a Title

Circle the best title for each picture.

1.

   Riding a Seahorse

   Going for a Ride

2.

   Mice Like Cheese

   Dinner Time

3.

   A Skater's Bad Fall

   The Ice Skater

4.

   Turtles Are Funny

   The Skating Turtle

Main Ideas

Circle the main idea for each story.

1. It's fun to climb. Big trees are the best. I pull myself up to the biggest branch. Then down I swing.

   a. Swinging
   b. Climbing Trees
   c. Up and Down

2. I'm going to make cookies today. It's fun. I mix everything in a bowl. Then onto a pan and into the oven they go!

   a. Baking Cookies
   b. Cooking
   c. Making a Cake

3. My dad came to our school today. He told us all about his job. All the kids asked him questions. My teacher did, too.

   a. My Father
   b. Schoolwork
   c. Dad's School Visit

Summer Fun

Read each story. Circle the title that gives the main idea.

1. We are going to the big pool today. I'm going to learn to swim. My lessons will be on Monday, Wednesday, and Friday for two weeks.

   a. Fun at the Pool
   b. Swimming Lessons

2. Do you know what I like about summer? Going to the movies! Mom took us last week, and we get to go again today. I love movies!

   a. Summer Movies
   b. School Is Out

3. Our family is going on a camping trip. We will put up our big tent. Our sleeping bags go inside. We get to camp for a week!

   a. Camping Out
   b. Putting Up the Tent

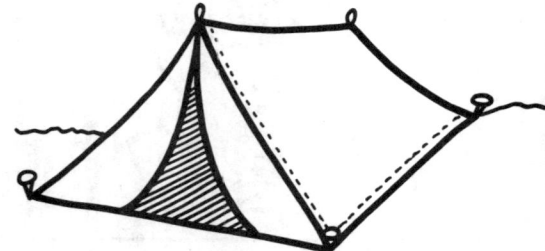

4. Brandy, our dog, loves dog bones. She will sit up to get one. Then she barks two times. It's fun to feed her.

   a. Dogs
   b. Dog Bones for Brandy

Could it happen? Circle 👍 or 👎   Yes   No

1. A dog could build a house.

2. A girl could play soccer.

3. An airplane could fly.

4. A horse could run on clouds.

5. A bird could turn into a boy.

6. You could have three birthdays in a year.

7. A man could drive a car.

8. It could rain popcorn balls.

9. You could talk on a phone.

10. A boy could run five miles.

Draw a line from the riddle to the right picture.

What am I?

1. I live in the desert
   I have a big hump.
   I can go for days
   without water.

2. I am long and low.
   I live in the water.
   Watch out for my jaws
   or I may eat you!

3. I am tall.
   My neck is long.
   I can eat leaves
   from tall trees.

4. I have a mane.
   I can roar.
   I am the King of
   the Jungle.

5. I am black and white.
   I have stripes.
   I look something like
   a horse.

What happened next? Circle the right answer.

1. Jan kicked the soccer ball down the left side of the field. The goalie moved to the left side of the net. Jan knew what she had to do to score.
   a. Jan kicked to the right side of the net.
   b. Jan threw the ball to a teammate.

2. Bob saw something moving in the bushes. An animal walked onto the path in front of him. It was black and white. Bob did the smart thing.
   a. Bob grabbed for the animal
   b. Bob backed away slowly.

3. It was a nice, hot day. Cathy was going on the water slide. She walked up the big hill. She waited in line a short time.
   a. Cathy walked back down.
   b. Cathy went down the water slide.

Porcupines

Have you ever seen a porcupine? I hope you didn't try to pick him up. Those long, sharp things sticking out of his body are called quills. If the porcupine moves his tail near anything soft, like an animal, one of his sharp quills may stick into the animal. The quill stays in because of a small barb on the end of it. One small quill can stick in the skin of a large animal. After a long time, the quill could work its way into the animal's body and even kill it. If a quill sticks to you, be sure to pull it out!

Circle the best answer for each question.

1. What kinds of things do quills stick to?
   hard   soft   dirt

2. What is the **barb** of a quill?
   animal   middle   hook

3. What is a good title?
   A Sticky Subject   Making Quills   Big Animals

4. What would happen first?
   A quill works its way into a bear's skin.
   A bear gets stuck with a quill.

5. A porcupine is small...
   ...so it is afraid of big animals.
   ...but it can take care of itself.
   ...and fun to play with.

Skunks

Would you like to have a skunk as a pet? They are really very friendly animals. Just be sure to have its oil sac taken out first! The sac is by his tail. If something scares a skunk, he just lifts up his tail and sprays the oil. The smell is terrible! That's why animals and people stay away from skunks.

Fill in the answers.

1. What does a skunk spray?

2. Where is the oil sac?

3. Why does a skunk spray?

4. What would be a better title?

5. If someone has a pet skunk, what has been done to the skunk?

Light and Sight

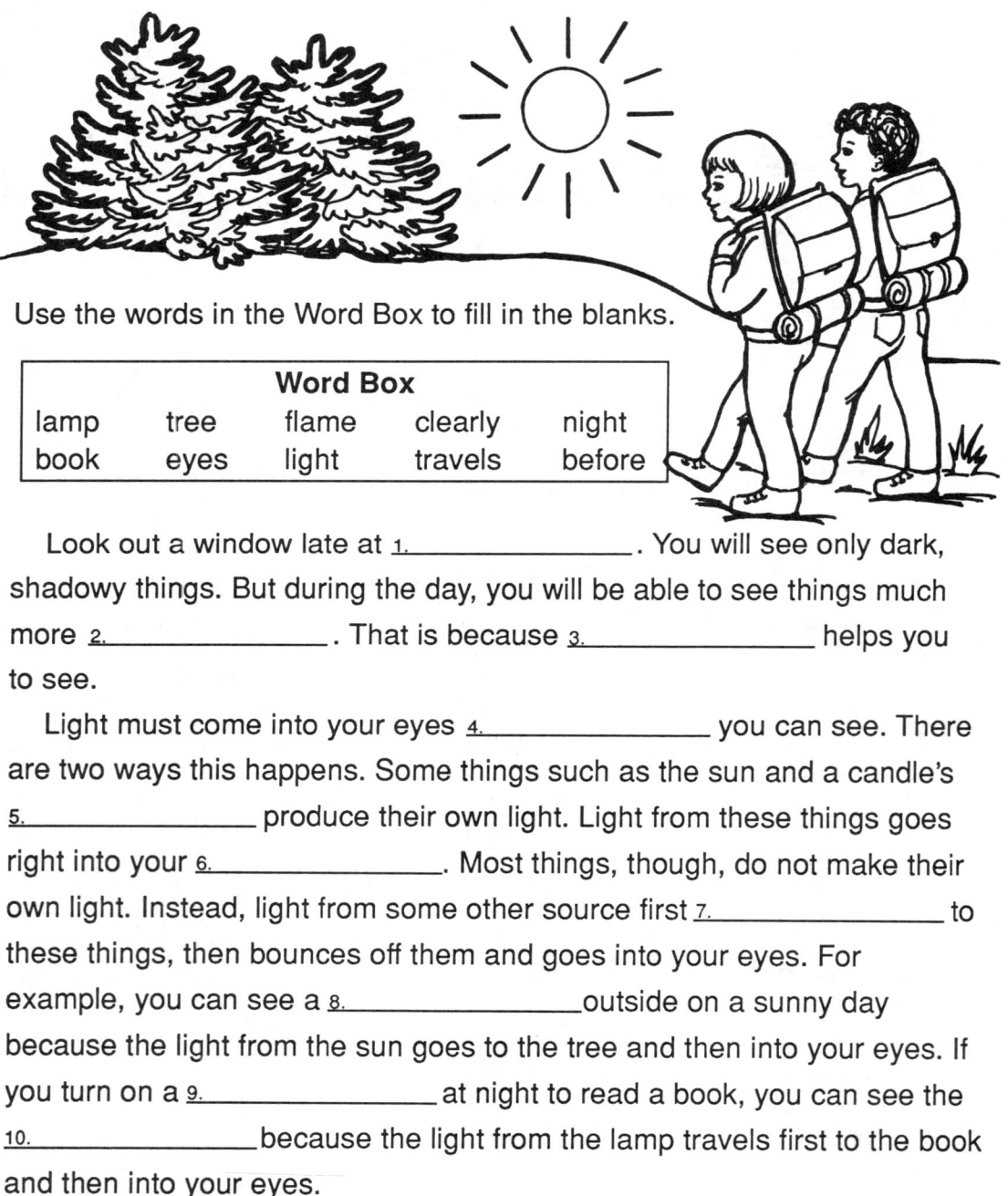

Use the words in the Word Box to fill in the blanks.

Word Box

lamp	tree	flame	clearly	night
book	eyes	light	travels	before

Look out a window late at 1._____. You will see only dark, shadowy things. But during the day, you will be able to see things much more 2._____. That is because 3._____ helps you to see.

Light must come into your eyes 4._____ you can see. There are two ways this happens. Some things such as the sun and a candle's 5._____ produce their own light. Light from these things goes right into your 6._____. Most things, though, do not make their own light. Instead, light from some other source first 7._____ to these things, then bounces off them and goes into your eyes. For example, you can see a 8._____ outside on a sunny day because the light from the sun goes to the tree and then into your eyes. If you turn on a 9._____ at night to read a book, you can see the 10._____ because the light from the lamp travels first to the book and then into your eyes.

Try This! What provides light in your classroom? Draw a picture of it.

Homework Helper Record

Color the bean for each page you complete.

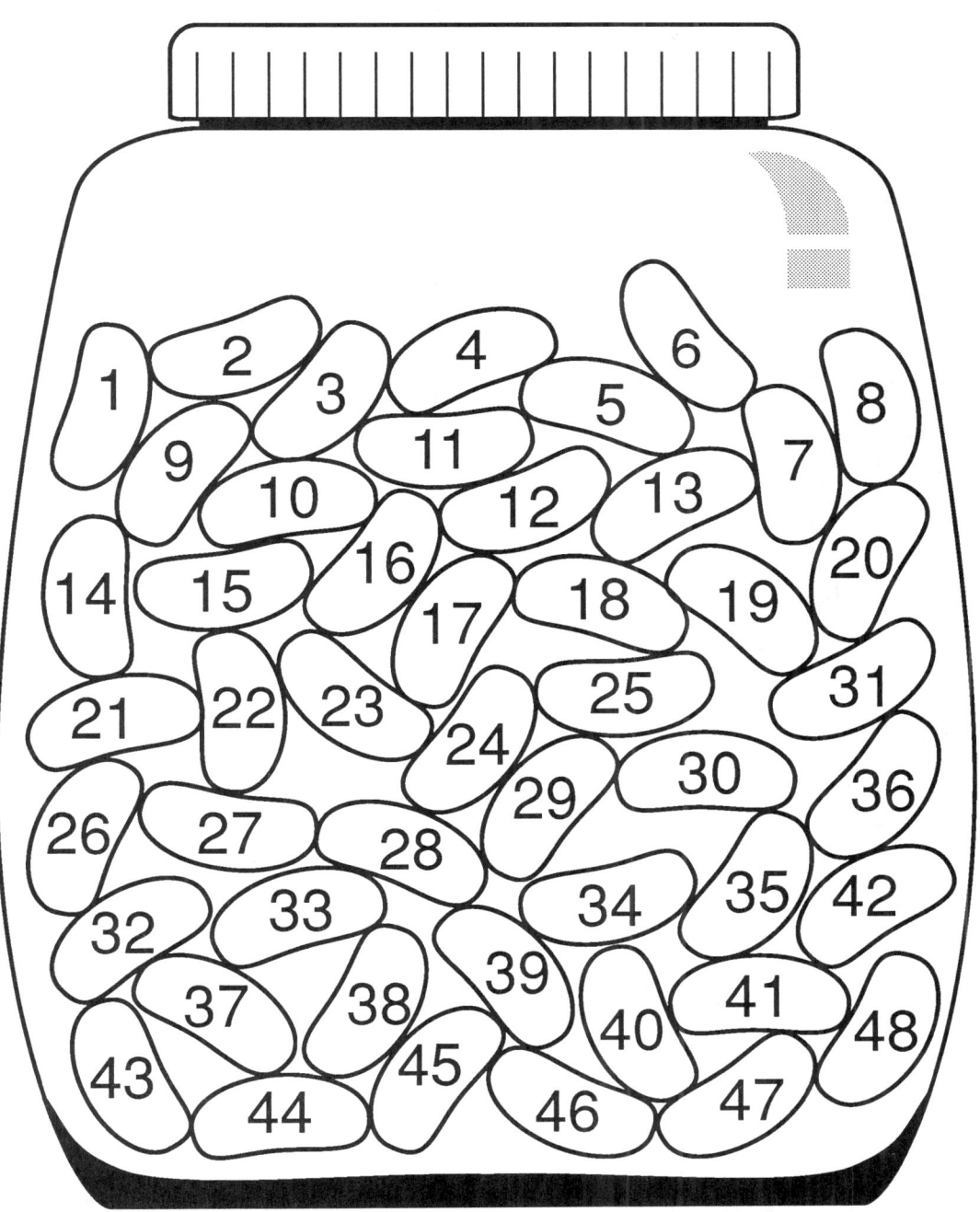